At the Pumpkin Patch

Katie Peters

GRL Consultant Diane Craig,
Certified Literacy Specialist

Lerner Publications ◆ Minneapolis

Lerner Publications
An imprint of Lerner Publishing Group, Inc.
241 First Avenue North
Minneapolis, MN 55401 USA

For reading levels and more information, look up this title at www.lernerbooks.com.

Main body text set in Memphis Pro 24/39
Typeface provided by Linotype.

Photo Acknowledgments
The images in this book are used with the permission of: © Clari Massimiliano/Shutterstock Images, p. 3; © Eltonlaw/Shutterstock Images, pp. 4–5, 16 (barn); © Vera Zinkova/ Shutterstock Images, pp. 6–7; © fritz16/Shutterstock Images, pp. 8–9, 16 (tractor); © K Hanley CHDPhoto/Shutterstock Images, pp. 10–11; © Michael Warwick/Shutterstock Images, pp. 12–13, 16 (scarecrow); © kali9/iStockphoto, pp. 14–15.

Front Cover: © SmoothSailing/Shutterstock Images

Library of Congress Cataloging-in-Publication Data

Names: Peters, Katie, author.
Title: At the pumpkin patch / by Katie Peters.
Description: Minneapolis : Lerner Publications, [2024] | Series: Let's look at fall (pull ahead readers - nonfiction) | Includes index. | Audience: Ages 4–7 | Audience: Grades K–1 | Summary: "Colorful photographs and leveled text invite readers to see all the fun things that they can find at the pumpkin patch. Pairs with the fiction book Tractor Ride"— Provided by publisher.
Identifiers: LCCN 2022033293 (print) | LCCN 2022033294 (ebook) | ISBN 9781728491301 (library binding) | ISBN 9798765603154 (paperback) | ISBN 9781728498027 (ebook)
Subjects: LCSH: Pumpkin—Juvenile literature. | Autumn—Juvenile literature. | Readers (Primary)
Classification: LCC SB347 .P43 2024 (print) | LCC SB347 (ebook) | DDC 635/.62—dc23/eng/20220719

LC record available at https://lccn.loc.gov/2022033293
LC ebook record available at https://lccn.loc.gov/2022033294

Manufactured in the United States of America
1 – CG – 7/15/23

Table of Contents

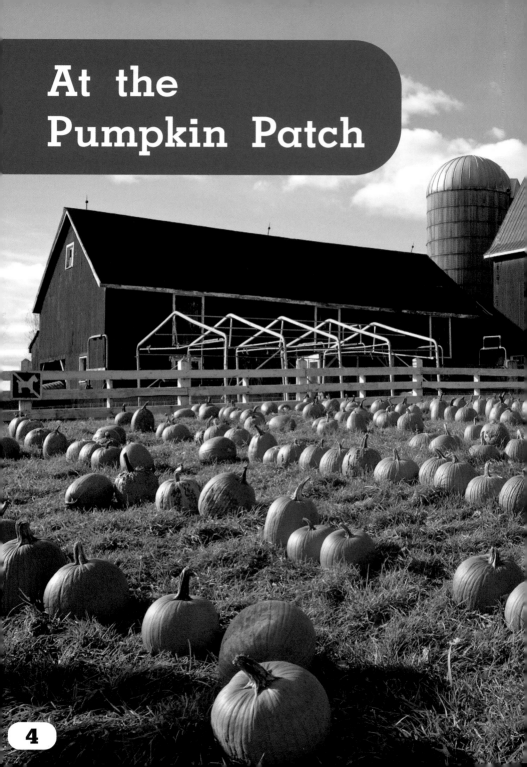

At the Pumpkin Patch

I see a barn.

I see a pony.

I see a tractor.

I see a wagon.

I see a scarecrow.

I see pumpkins!

What would you like to see at a pumpkin patch?

Did You See It?

barn   scarecrow   tractor

Index